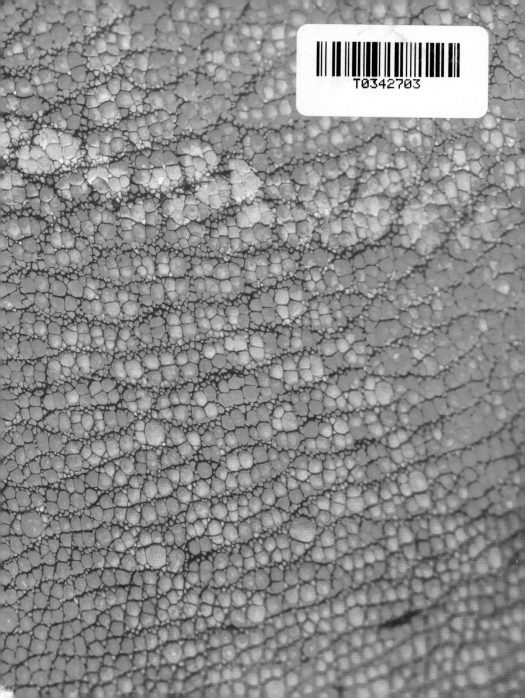

DID YOU KNOW?

Lizards

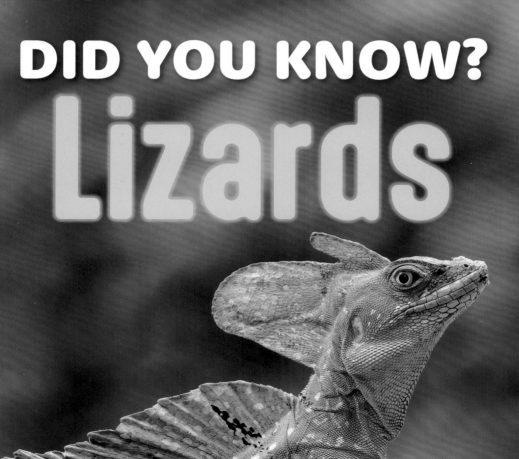

DID YOU KNOW?
Lizards

young reed

Contents

A lizard that looks like a snake!
This is a Common Scaly-foot from Australia.

What is a Lizard?

- Lizards are **reptiles** that have scaly skin.

- Together with snakes, lizards belong to the order called **Squamata**.

- Lizards can usually — but not always — be distinguished from snakes because they have **legs** and **moving eyelids**.

Most lizards have eyelids, but not geckos, which instead clean their eyes using their long tongue.

What's NOT a Lizard?

Although they look similar, none of the animals shown here are lizards...

● **Dinosaurs** were not lizards — although they were reptiles they belonged to a different family called **Archosaurs**.

● Today's **Crocodiles** are also **Archosaurs**, so they are more closely related to the dinosaurs than to lizards.

● Although many **Newts** and **Salamanders** look like lizards, they have smooth or bumpy skin, rather than scales, and belong to the **Amphibian** family. Also, their young grow up underwater and look like tadpoles.

● Although **Tuataras** look like lizards, they are from a different ancient reptile family. Today they survive only in New Zealand.

● The **Common Lizard** of Europe and Asia can survive in cold conditions right up into the **Arctic Circle**. It gives birth to **live young** rather than lay eggs which could chill.

● The largest family of lizards is the **skinks**, with more than **one thousand species**.

Fire Skink.

Common Lizard.

Amazing adaptations

● Most lizards are **cold-blooded**, meaning that they need heat from the sun or another source to warm them.

The process of growing a new tail.

● Some lizards will **shed their tail** to help escape from predators — this is called **autotomy**. In time they will **grow a new tail** from the stump.

Black-and-white Tegu.

● At least one species — the **Black-and-white Tegu from South America** — has been found to be **warm-blooded** like mammals and birds.

Big and small

- Growing to more than **three metres** in length, the **Komodo Dragon** from Indonesia is the largest lizard in the world.

- These dragons are **carnivores** and **apex predators** — they feed on prey as large as pigs and water buffalo.

Komodo Dragon.

● The world's smallest lizard is the *Brookesia nana* **chameleon** from Madagascar. A fully grown adult will fit comfortably on to a **human fingernail.**

Brookesia nana chameleon.

Weird and wonderful

Marine Iguana.

● **Chameleons** are among the most amazing of all lizards. They can **change colour** to match their background, and each **eye swivels independently** of the other.

● **Marine Iguanas** swim in the ocean, feed on algae and even drink seawater, snorting out the salt through their nostrils!

● The bright colours of the **Gila Monster** warn that it is a **venomous** lizard.

Gila Monster.

Panther Chameleon looking both ways.

Staying safe

● Some lizards, such as the **Thorny Devil** and **Horned Lizards,** have scales developed into **spines** to deter potential predators from eating them.

● Others try to surprise their enemies — for example, the blue-tongue skinks stick out their **bright blue tongues** to make predators think twice before having them for dinner.

Blue-tongue skink.

Thorny Devil.

● Perhaps the most amazing display is that of the **Frilled Lizard**, which raises a **ruff of skin** around its head to make it look bigger and more intimidating.

● Chameleons can **change colour** to blend in with their background, using **camouflage** to avoid predators.

Frilled Lizard.

Chameleon blending in with its background.

What's for dinner?

● It all depends on the size of the lizard! Many eat small **insects**, some eat **plants**, and big monitor lizards can eat **animals** as large as monkeys or even deer.

The catapult tongue of a Chameleon.

Monitor lizards are carnivores.

- The Chameleon shoots out its **sticky tongue** like a **catapult** to catch bugs.

- Geckos use their special foot-pads to **walk upside-down** on ceilings to find insect prey.

Gecko foot-pads.

Family life

● Many lizard species **lay eggs** — these species are known as **oviparous**.

● Other species give birth to **live young** — they are described as **viviparous**.

● All young lizards — whether born or hatched — look like **miniature versions** of the adults.

● Some lizard parents **care for their young** for a few months, while the babies of other species have to look after themselves straight away.

Blue-tailed Skink female tending eggs at a nest.

Young iguana hatching from an egg.

First published in 2025 by
New Holland Publishers
Sydney

newhollandpublishers.com

Level 1, 178 Fox Valley Road, Wahroonga, NSW 2076, Australia

A record of this book is held at the National Library of Australia.

ISBN 978 1 92107 388 5

OTHER TITLES IN THE 'DID YOU KNOW?' SERIES:

Kangaroos
ISBN 978 1 92107 386 1

Koala
ISBN 978 1 92107 387 8

Meerkat
ISBN 978 1 92107 389 2

Penguins
ISBN 978 1 92107 390 8

Red Panda
ISBN 978 1 92107 391 5

For details of these books and hundreds
of other Natural History titles see
newhollandpublishers.com